this book belongs to:

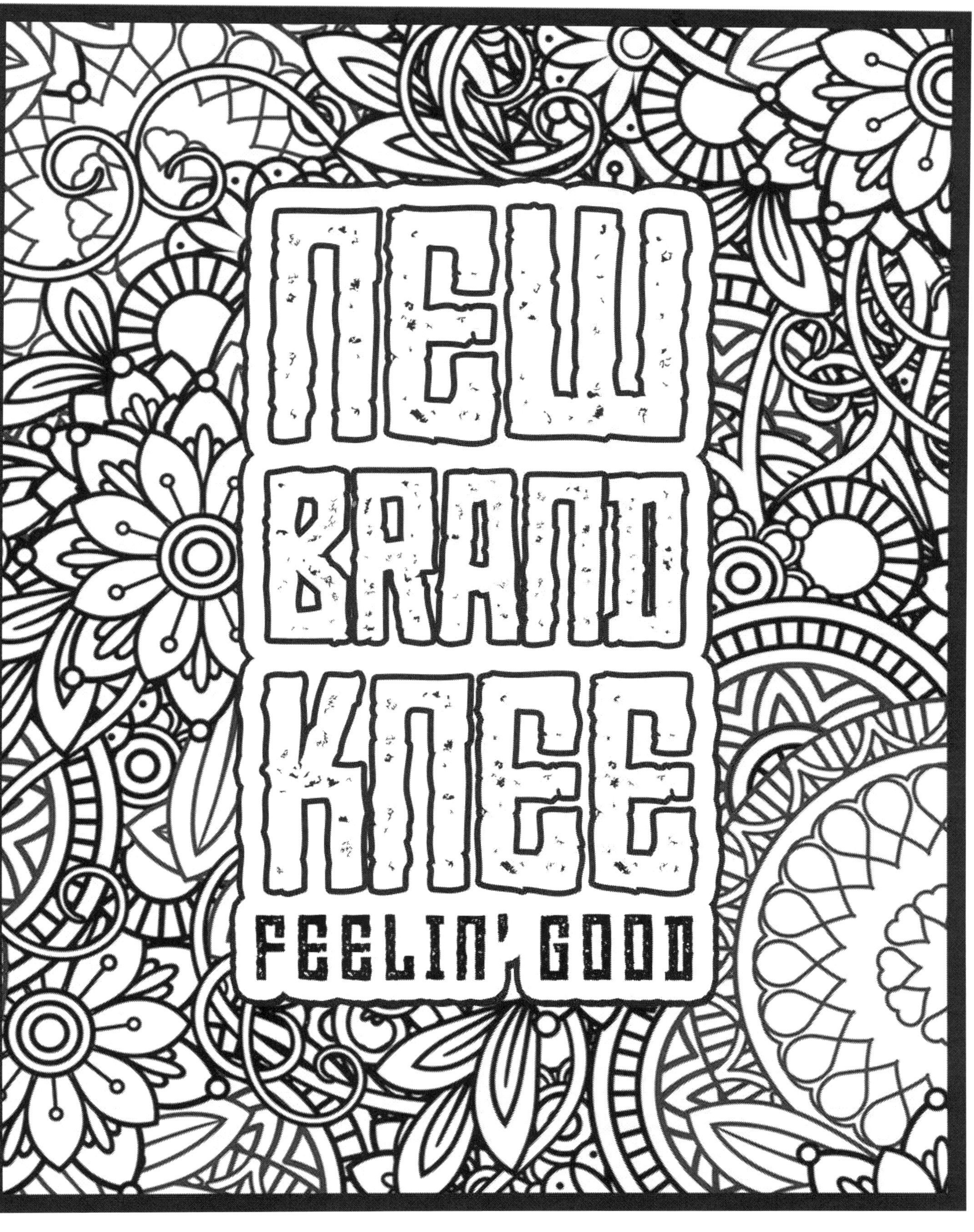
NEW
BRAND
KNEE
FEELIN' GOOD

!CAUTION!
KNEE SURGERY
RECOVERY
IN PROGRESS

New
Knee
New
Me

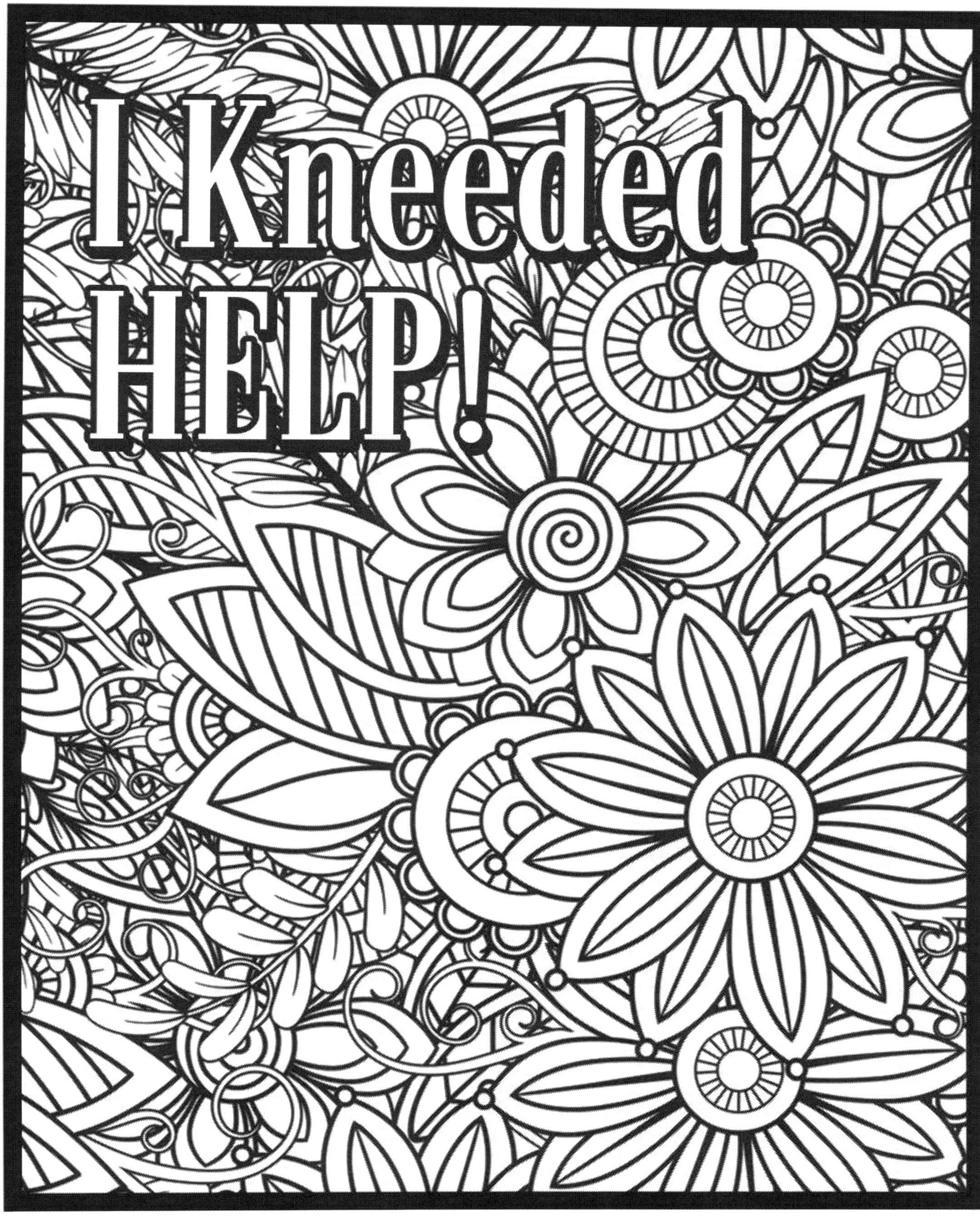
I Kneeded
HELP!

Knee Surgery?
No Prob-
Llama

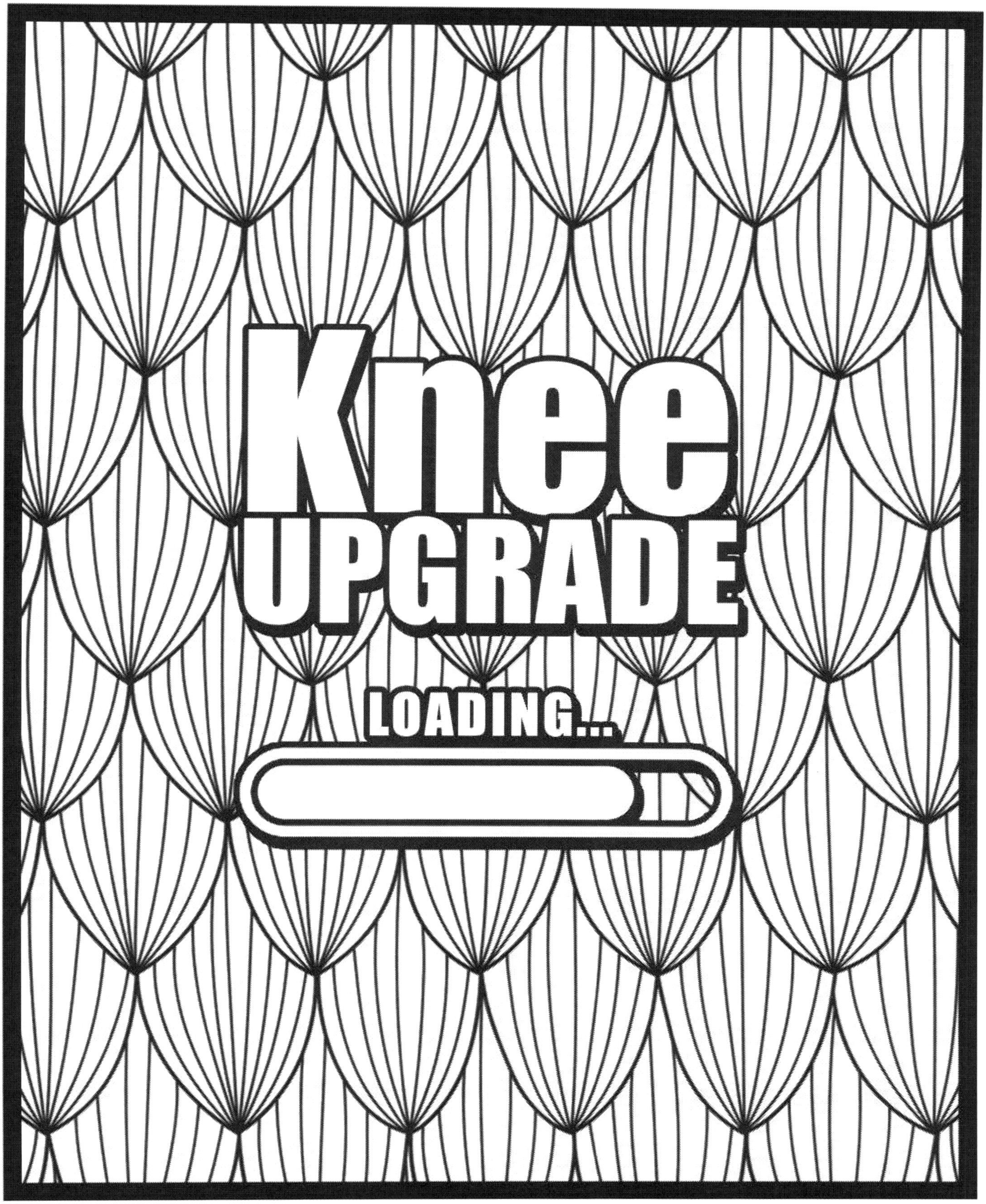
Knee
UPGRADE
LOADING...

SURGERY
SURVIVOR

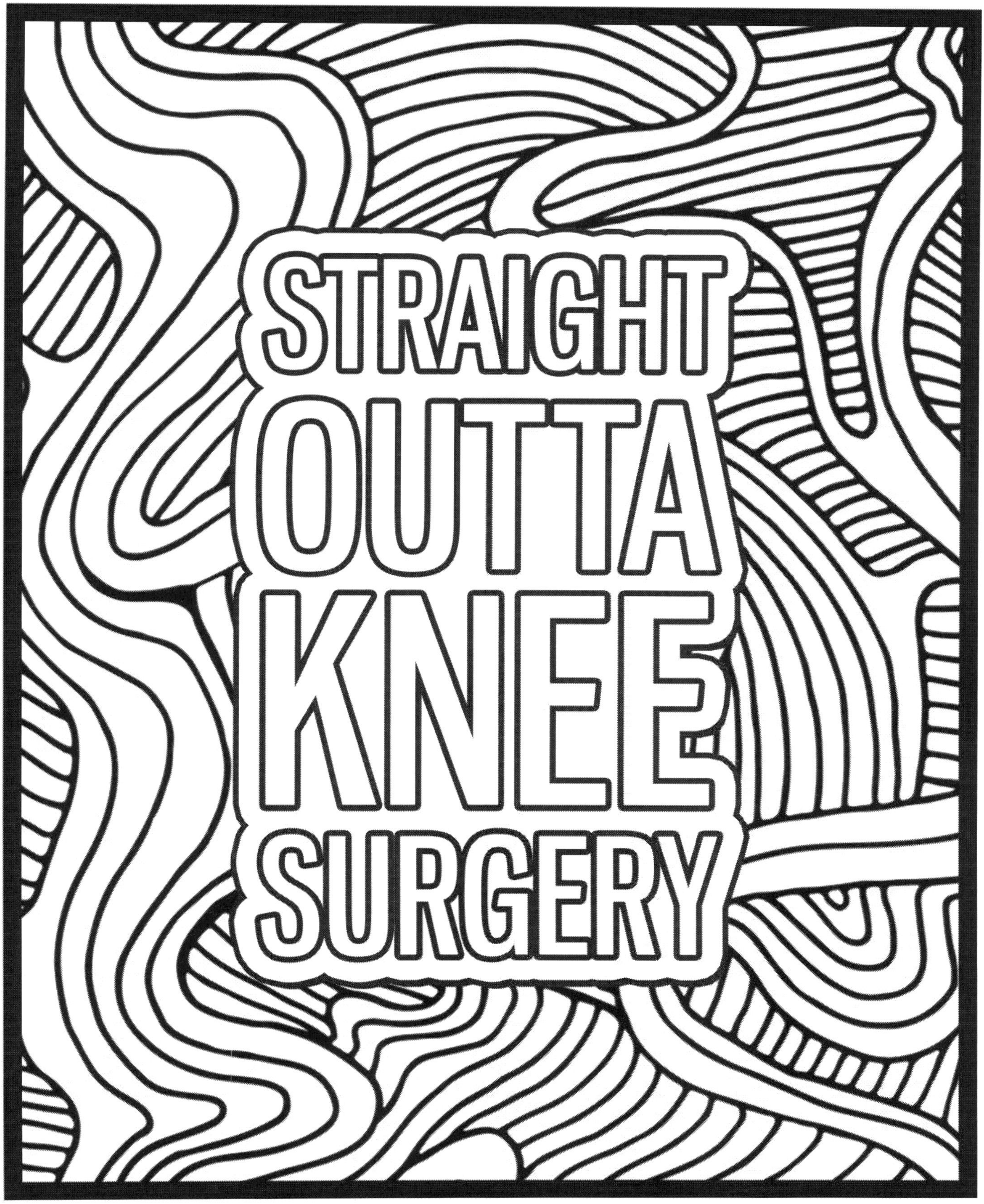
STRAIGHT
OUTTA
KNEE
SURGERY

I Love
My New
Knee

Just a minor
Setback
For a major
Comeback

MAKE MY
KNEE
GREAT
AGAIN

NOT EVEN A
SURGERY
CAN STOP
ME!

Happiness
is a new
Knee

GET WELL
SOON!

my knee
isn't new
it's
certified
refurbished

RECOVERY
MODE
ON!

TODAY'S GOOD
MOOD IS BROUGHT
TO YOU BY MY
NEW
KNEE

DOES MY
NEW KNEE
MAKE ME
LOOK
SEXY?

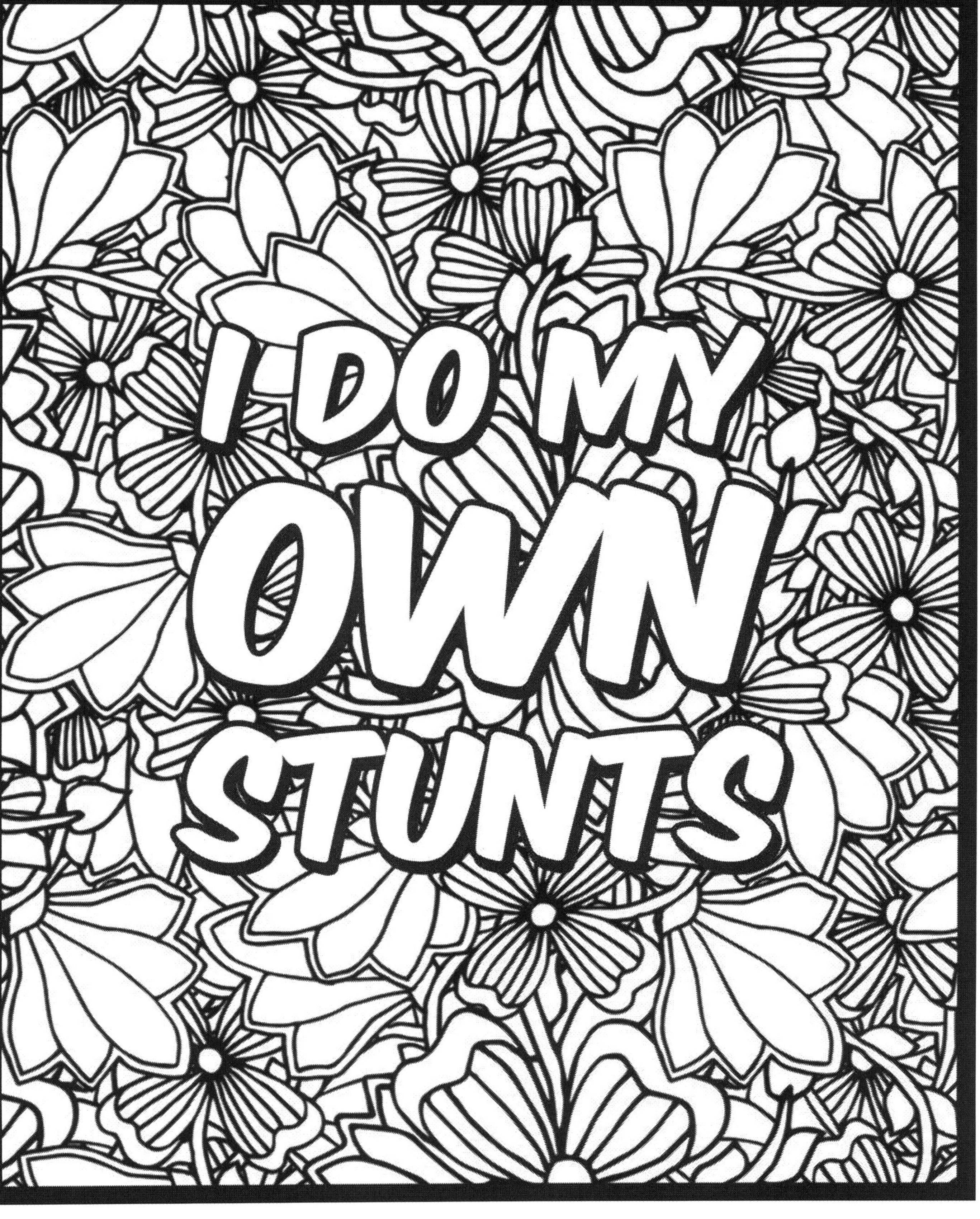
I DO MY
OWN
STUNTS

Knee Surgery?
I Call it
Performance
Upgrade

Made in the USA
Columbia, SC
14 March 2025

55176084R00024